T0209496

JESUS FOCUSED LIFE

LIVING AND LEADING WITH A PURPOSE

COREY GIBSON

WESTBOW
PRESS®
A DIVISION OF THOMAS NELSON
& ZONDERVAN

WestBow Press books may be ordered through booksellers or by contacting:

WestBow Press
A Division of Thomas Nelson & Zondervan
1663 Liberty Drive
Bloomington, IN 47403
www.westbowpress.com
1 (866) 928-1240

Cover art design by Johnathan Key

ISBN: 978-1-9736-5239-7 (sc)
ISBN: 978-1-9736-5238-0 (e)

Print information available on the last page.

WestBow Press rev. date: 03/15/2019

CONTENTS

ABOUT THE AUTHOR

Pastor Corey Gibson has been involved in full-time ministry for the past 14+ years. He is an ordained Pastor and has a passion for ministering to young people. He has been preaching & leading since the age of 8 years old, as a young volunteer servant leader at Victory World Church (Atlanta, GA). Growing up as a Pastor's Kid, he knew that ministry would be a part of his DNA. Currently, Corey is the Executive Pastor at Transformation Life Church in Murfreesboro, Tennessee as well as an itinerate speaker who travels preaching the gospel of Jesus through his 501(c)3 nonprofit, Corey Gibson Ministries. Alongside leading and ministering at his home church full-time, he also speaks at various conferences, camps, school assemblies and other events as time permits. He has spoken to thousands of young people in his 14+ years of ministry with the message of the saving Gospel of Jesus Christ. He is dedicated to igniting citywide revivals wherever and whenever he travels to preach the Gospel. He considers it an honor to be used by God as a carrier of the Gospel and watchmen on the walls.

His burning desires is that this generation would respond to the Cross and embrace (encounter/experience) Grace, which is the personification, revelation and embodiment of Jesus! His dream is to build and passionately lead in the local church while investing and developing leaders, both students and adults, empowering them to do the ministry of the church. His vision and mission are simple: To see generations of people, young and old, have a life-changing encounter with God, which causes a revolutionary movement of changed lives for the cause of Christ!

"Being a Generation that is Responding to the Cross and Embracing Grace"

INTRODUCTION

*"I pray we never lead without urgency and grace or never work without faith and hope. May we never stop loving people until Jesus returns. Finally, may we never lose our awe and wonder in/of Jesus!" @ meCoreyG #ForMe #ForYou #**JesusFocusedLife** #Leadership*

This all started the Spring of 2014 when I would post on social media with the *hashtag* #JesusFocusedLife. I was led of the Lord to begin posting on things that would lead us to focus on Jesus despite our circumstances. This #JesusFocusedLife picked up with some friends and followers. It became a movement of sorts and out of that, I was posting blogs or journals on the Jesus focused leadership and life experiences I was living.

This book is about life… a life that is focused on Jesus and his mission. It is a collection of journals and stories of life lessons I've learned in my time with full-time ministry. *Jesus Focused Life* will make you cry, laugh, think critically and spiritually, question God, and be in awe of the redemptive nature of

Jesus. My prayer is that you open your heart and embrace all that God is speaking to you through reading *Jesus Focused Life*. Regardless if you are a pastor, volunteer leader, business executive, professional, parent or student - this *Jesus Focused Life* is for you. May you embrace the call on your life as you focus more on Jesus and less on everything else.

The adventure awaits... will you make it count?

Corey Gibson
Pastor & Author,
Corey Gibson Ministries

DEDICATION

I am dedicating this book to all those who want to live and lead like Jesus in a society that is against the standards of the Gospel. For the ones who are tired of living a life for the applause of man and want to focus on Jesus. To the ones who want to grow in a deeper walk with God and lead at a higher capacity. No matter what's your walk in life as a church pastor or volunteer leaders, business person, teacher or student, parent, doctor or nurse, or just trying to figure it all out - I dedicate this book to YOU! May we live a life that is fashioned and inundated with Jesus.

13 THINGS IN 13 YEARS...
LEADERSHIP & LIFE

In the past 13 years, I have learned a lot and wanted to share with my readers and friends some of the most significant leadership principles and life lessons I've learned. Not by any means am I saying that I am perfect in all of these things, but it's something that I am consistently doing or improving in. All of life is a process of and for growth...

Jesus is Everything | Jesus is the main thing and matters more as we sojourn through life. He is the rhyme and reason for living. The centrality of all of life is found in him. Jesus is the one we worship, love and Gospel we teach/preach. He is the ONE we point people to. We give him pre-eminence as he has all authority and power. All that we do should be from an overflow of intimacy with Jesus and in faithful obedience to him. He is the only truth & way to salvation and hope in life. This is our first priority as leaders. Acts 17:2-3 | Colossians 1:15-23; 2:2-10; 3:1-4 | John 1:1-18; 14:1-14 | Luke 2:36-38

Trust the Voice of the Holy Spirit | Right before Jesus ascends to heaven to be at the right hand of the Father... he sends us the Holy Spirit. The leadership of the Holy Spirit is so crucial to the day to day life that we live. The Holy Spirit bestows gifts from the Father to us to live accordingly in regard to the Great Commission. We are also empowered to live according to the Gospel and commissioned to walk out the Sermon on the Mount as a lifestyle. We must subscribe to the leadership of the Holy Spirit!!! He is the leader Jesus gave us... so we must walk in his ways! Beloved, leave plenty of room for the Holy Spirit to move through your services and lives as he deals with our hearts. The Holy Spirit is actively alive as a person to Counsel, Convict, & Comfort Us. Acts 1:1-8; 2 | John 14:15-31; 16:5-15 | Luke 24:49

Define the WIN | As if to say... what's the purpose? As leaders and in life in general as well, we have to know the purpose to why we do whatever we do. No matter what it is, such as planning an event, preaching a sermon, running a business or partnering with an orphanage, the WIN is vital. This WIN keeps our focus, allows us to set goals and makes leading others easier. Vision, Mission, and Core Values all shape our WIN. Great questions to ask ourselves – "What is the WIN for my life, family, business or ministry/church?" Another question to ask – "How can I help someone else defined their WIN?

Authentic Community Matters | This is a big one for me. Simply put, the people you do life with matters. Your close friends and family, your spouse, your business partners, your mentor and the ones who speak directly into your life – all make up this authentic community. You get to choose who is in this community with you. BE CAREFUL who has an ear to your voice AND whose voice you have an ear to.

Your authentic community must have the right to support or champion, encourage, confront and correct you. Your community needs to be people who love and believes in you, not just what you do or what they can get out of you. God is a God of relationship and community. More about friendship and authentic community later on...

Rest well | The hated 4-letter word for a hard-worker. Often times, this is one of the hardest things to do especially when it relates to ministry and entrepreneurship. REST! We are called to rest as it's biblical. Our God, the Creator of the Universe, rested after creation. Most of the miracles of Jesus are surrounded by Jesus resting either before or after the miracle. When I think of resting well, I am always reminded of Psalm 127... Isn't it funny right before the fruit (offspring/children) comes from the man's labor, rest was a need. **Do not neglect the times of resting in the Lord.** In a society that always has a constant go and "move now" mentality, God is still calling us to rest. Even the battle in and of the mind makes us feel like we always have to be doing something, God calls us to rest. Make no mistake about it there are things to do, important things... but rest is needed in order for you to not burn out. You and I can rest in the finished work of the Cross. Interestingly enough... resting well requires being refreshed and being refreshed only comes from repenting as we spend quality time with Jesus. (Act 3:19-20)

Forgive quickly (Move forward) | Simply move forward from the hurt and pain. I have learned after several years in ministry just to let things go. Forgive quickly and move on as you free yourself from the burden. I love how Jesus handles no doubt with joy a moment of denial from Peter. He poetically tells Peter to keep the WIN alive by feeding Jesus' sheep (people).

The Bible never records Jesus seeking an apology from Peter for denying him or even Peter offering one up. They just moved forward with the mission. This is to say regardless if you ever get an 'I'm Sorry' or apology from the person that done you wrong — **FORGIVE & PRESS FORWARD IN YOUR MISSION. If you don't pain will cripple you to move forward and the weight of it all will crush you.**

Own the mistake/Failure isn't final | We have all been there and done something completely stupid. I mean like some really dumb off the walls things. We're humans after all. I'm personally all to acquainted with the apostle Paul's statement of doing what I don't want to do (Roman 7:15-20). If you make a mistake, own up to it and don't make excuses. Repent quickly and seek counsel, if need be, from a trusted friend. This is a sign of a true leader. Leaders are willing to take responsibility even if it's not wrongdoing of theirs. Likewise, we will all fail at something. You are not your failure. It doesn't have to define you and keep you in chains or bondage. Break free from it by owning the failed thing and admitting to it. Failure is not your identity and it isn't final! *"TRANSPARENCY… light can only shine through something that's transparent."* – Chad Veach // Side note: True leaders also *at times* own the mistake of others so that they don't have to bear the guilt, shame, exposure, and punishment. Don't believe me… look no further than Jesus himself and the Cross. We are all recipients of this.

Be Guarded | Sure this one could have fit under "Authentic Community Matters" but this is so important that I had to make it a separate point. GUARD your time, heart, and yes. Are you married, guard your marriage/spouse? Those with kids, guard family time. This is not about a defensive strategy, but rather an offensive tool and protection. You must protect yourself. The right yes, to the wrong person or time, is so damaging as a leader. Develop personal boundaries and create personnel policies/procedures for this. We as leaders must strategically cultivate the "art of no" so that we can produce the "fruit of yes." I remembered 12 years ago, I had a massive opportunity at an amazing church, but I turned it down, to protect my character. Often, we think of faith as saying yes to impossible things. We also need to look at it as saying no to something great, because we know God has something better. This is hard but needed as a leader.

Be faithful & faith-filled | Are you found in the house of being consistent and then filled with faith? Like when people describe you, do loyal, supportive, constant and steadfast come to mind? How about a person who just believes the absolute best of an impossible situation? These two character traits are so crucial to a person as they set the trajectory of your life and calling. Be faithful in your time, resources and friendship. Be faith-filled to the point where people look at you a little crazy because overwhelming hope and joy are displayed. Surround yourself with these types of people… it is contagious!

Honor unconditionally | I know, I know… we like the *honor* part but dislike the *unconditionally* part. It's hard, so I really do get it. But if we want to lead well, we must also honor well. How's your honor in public AND in private??? This could make all the difference. How about your honoring even when it's not reciprocated? *"Honor is vital in the Kingdom. A culture of honor that seeks to uplift and encourage others produces superb growth conditions." – Graham Cooke*

Enjoy the journey | Life is but a vapor… here one moment and gone the next. Enjoy the journey God has you on, no matter if it wasn't what you expected or schemed up in 7th grade. I promise you, the adventures God has you on is better than anything you wanted for yourself.

Pray always. Worship always. | Prayer has the power to make ordinary men and women, extraordinary, SO PRAY. No matter the season of life, and no matter the circumstances – Prayer and worship ALWAYS win. I have personally talked myself out of crazy things just by praying or rocking out to worship. When life gets you down… worship lifts you up.

- *If we fail in prayer, we fail everywhere. – Pastor Daniel Gray*
- *Any sermon that is not birthed in prayer is not a message from God no matter how learned the preacher.* A.W. Tozer
- *If God answered all your prayers would it change the world or just your world?* – Pastor Chris Hodges
- *Worship is our response to what we value most. As a result, worship fuels our actions, becoming the driving force of all we do.* – Pastor Louie Giglio
- *Your worship provokes victory.* - Pastor Johnathan Key
- *Worship reminds us who God is and who we are. As our soul worships, we stay level, grounded in God, and become our authentic selves.* – Pastor Judah Smith

Comparison kills | Maybe one of the most dangerous things we can do in ministry is to allow the comparison game to get the best of us. This game is consumed with jealousy/envy, vanity, friendly fire and unhealthy need for competition. The church/ministry, event, and leader are not in competition with me and what I am doing. We are on the same team. Yes, it is wise to see what others are doing and how they are doing it.

Sure "borrow" an idea or fifty-two… but obsessing with their model, their size, their leadership focus/style, and their arts/media is super unhealthy. I cannot help but wonder even in my own life how much this comparison shapes my thinking. Every time I get on Instagram or Facebook and see the latest, I wonder how damaging it is to my own soul seeing well-meaning people I admire doing things I want or dream of doing. If you and I aren't careful, we will end up wishing we were someone else and lose focus on our calling, gifts, and purpose. We all have a race that we have to run, but I can't run my race while watching yours in your lane. Longevity in ministry, life, and general leadership is paved when we get our focus off of others and back on God and the WIN. More to come on this in the next chapter.

THE WAR AGAINST COMPARISON

> *The comparison game is a losing battle that will leave*
> *you wounded and in disobedience! - @meCoreyG*

TCGWKY: Battle 1

The letters TCGWKY represent "The Comparison Game Will Kill You." It comes from the thought based out of my 13 things in 13 years found in chapter 1, specifically #13 – Comparison Kills.

This is what I wrote in the previous chapter…

#13 – Comparison Kills: Maybe one of the most dangerous things we can do in ministry is to allow the comparison game to get the best of us. This game is consumed with jealousy/envy, vanity, friendly fire and an unhealthy need for competition. The church/ministry, event, and leader are not in competition with me and what I am doing. We are on the same team. Yes, it is wise to see what others are doing and how they are doing it. Sure "borrow" an idea or fifty-two… but obsessing with their model, their size, their leadership focus/style, and their arts/media is super unhealthy. I cannot help but wonder even in my own life how much this comparison shapes my thinking. Every time I get on Instagram or Facebook and see the latest, I wonder how damaging it is to my own soul seeing well-meaning people I admire doing things I want or dream of doing. If you and I aren't careful, we will end up wishing we were someone else and lose focus on our calling, gifts, and purpose. We all have a race that we have to run, but I can't run my race while watching yours in your lane. Longevity in ministry, life, and general leadership is paved when we get our focus off of others and back on God and the WIN.

I want to expound on this a little more...

The comparison game is a killer to the health of a leader. It steals the joy and passion for the very purpose that leader has. Comparison is a constant nagger causing vision, purpose, and faith to be called into question continuously. It can destroy friendships and partnership. Lastly, it also seeks to eat at the mental health of a leader. This deadly game has become game over for a lot of people. In my honest opinion, it is the greatest threat to a spiritual leader. It is one of Satan's favorite snares and tools to use in destroying a pastor and any other type of leader.

When we begin to compare negatively... we are essentially telling God that what he is doing in us, is not better than what he is doing in someone else. We look at their status and position, their numbers/size, giving/sales, social media friends/followers, their likes/comments, and their everyday merely losing focus on the God-moments that is happening within our own lives. Often times, the clear indicator of being a character or player in the comparison game is the unwillingness to celebrate others and/or the feeling of not having enough in relations to others. THE COMPARISON GAME IS A LOSING BATTLE THAT WILL LEAVE YOU WOUNDED, LONELY AND IN DISOBEDIENCE!

This played out too well in the life of King Saul, who was filled with unbridled jealousy and enviousness. He saw David as a threat simply hearing silly girls chant "Saul kills his thousands, and David his ten thousands." This little melody started a saga of hatred and attempted murders. It snowballed and ultimately landed David as King and Saul dead.

Really think about your life and ministry... like really think about it. Are you seemingly playing in this game of negative comparison, losing sight of your identity, your vision, and your race you are running? Are you more concern with what others are doing instead of what you are doing? How's your motive when you look at others and what they are doing? Can you celebrate them without the "I wish that was me" or "I can do that, too?"

A moment of transparency... In the Spring and Summer of 2017, this comparison game and struggle had got the best of me. I saw a lot of my friends I personally know succeeding in life, relationships, and ministry, while I felt stuck in a transitional holding pattern. Some days my heart ached to have an incredible highlight reel of life, always on the go, traveling, speaking, being creative and simply enjoying. I came face to face with this comparison monster in July of 2017 which caused me to take close introspection of my life, refocus on Jesus, and pursue my dreams and calling deeply. So, I decided to get rid of what had caused most of this – SOCIAL MEDIA! I took some considerable time off of all social media just to get focus on the things that matter the most, Jesus and me. More time spent in worship and in prayer, more time in character building, and more time doing the intentional stuff for my life. It led me to a beautiful time of redefining my passions and is the catalyst to why you are reading this book now. Without this social media & internet sabbatical, I would have never spent the time planning, writing and developing this book.

My encouragement for everyone is to take inventory of your life and remove the comparison between you and someone else. Find joy and hope in the things that you are doing. Celebrate wins of the other people, encourage someone when they are down and embrace this journey of life God has you on… it's on purpose for a purpose.

TCGWKY: Battle 2

In just the last few years, I've been in three distinctly different seasons of life and ministry. I've been in the role of leading a ministry that was "small." I've been in the wilderness of transition, and I've been in the driver's seat of a nationally recognized movement. The idea that the spirit of comparison is exclusive, or even stronger, in any season is just as rich of a lie as that destructive sirens' promise that better grass exists. When I worked with a small ministry, I wanted to be in a bigger one. When I was in transition, I just wanted to be wanted, the way I felt everyone else who had a platform was... wanted. And when I had somehow "arrived" into my dream position, piloting a ministry that had influenced me for years, I was still just as empty and green as I had ever been. Shades of inadequacy and hues of envy colored the way I viewed everything.

I have watched friends fall at my left side and brothers abandon calling at my right hand. Moreover, in my most vulnerable moments, I can tell you that the same spirit has not just come nigh my dwelling, she has kissed my ear on my couch as I gaze into an iPhone wondering when I will ever "matter." She has taken my place in bed, next to my wife, while I pace through hallways and try to develop ideas like adding rungs onto a proverbial ladder. I've read enough books, listened to enough podcasts, and even preached enough sermons about not comparing people's highlight reels to your life. It's easy to say "Amen" to, but seemingly impossible to escape.

I chased success like some mythical white beast, that was always just far enough from my hands that I would never really reach it. I found myself constantly pursuing something other than the pursuer, and you simply can't live like that. All in all, I found myself subscribed to the idea that working harder was the answer. There's nothing wrong with hard work, but my every movement became about proving something to someone. I didn't care much who it was, but I had an intrinsic need for validation that was achingly insufficient – all because my life didn't look like the Instagram feeds that I had idolized. All because twitter followers somehow eluded me but migrated to everyone else. Because I couldn't for the life of me gain a blue check on Facebook. Because I only got to speak at four camps per summer, and not ten.

There's a reason it feels like you are always chasing... running and gasping for each breath, holding your ribs in exhaustion. Because comparison **never** wants to you to know satisfaction. No matter how big the ministry, how influential your social clout, how perfect your airbrushed photos are, there will always be another dying star that vies for your attention. And if we do not make a conscious choice to abdicate comparison's power of our life, we will make our spiritual dwelling in the slums of rejection.

Why? Because comparison and rejection are winning dance partners, and our western-progressive-Christian minds are the ballroom. A month ago, I found myself back in this place of transition. This time not just in employment, but in calling, in residence, in economic status, what felt like every aspect of life. At the pinnacle of this change, I laid in bed one night for hours listening to the same song on repeat. I lay there incessantly hitting "play again" all for a three-line bridge towards the end of the song where the singer says, "I'm gonna show what I've got left. You haven't even seen my best. Just wait." Somehow without me even noticing, years' worth of rejection began surfacing and I found myself weeping, gritting my teeth and bitterly declaring those three lines of lyrics over and over again.

All of that to say this, the comparison had made me believe that I would never live without being in someone else's shadow. A predecessor, a successor, an illegitimate idol who fits into skinny jeans better than I ever have hopes for, the list goes on...

That night I made a decision that the world would see my best. No matter what it took. I persuaded my own heart to trust that I still had something left inside to offer. The only way we kill comparison is regaining security in our God-given identity. Mine is different than yours. And it's different than my wife's. It's different than the pastor with 12,000 followers, and it's different than the guy who preaches in a living room for 12 people. We must come to a place where we unashamedly embrace our differences, where we celebrate the favor of God on our friends and on our rivals, where we cancel our premium subscription to Satan's lies and rejoice in who we are as children of God. I'm more and more convinced daily that genuine revival and comparison cannot cohabitate. The reason is, revival and comparison are at war for who gets the glory. If we authentically desire a move of God, the comparison must die.

- Pastor Johnathan Key

Johnathan is a speaker and church consultant with a passion for training leaders to "make things better, always." With 14 years of experience in ministry, Johnathan now travels spreading fires and coaching pastors, leaders, and volunteers to understand that revival is a choice. He is a husband to Andrea, dad to Israel, and Unashamed Skylanders collector.

WORTH IT ALL: OVERCOMING DIFFICULTIES

The person you are becoming is better than what you are doing now... Keep becoming who God has made you! Move toward Jesus. - @meCoreyG

The call to more and elevation is found in the Night season! Endure the darkness in order to get to the Light. - @meCoreyG

I Am Weak, That's Okay!

Ever since I could remember, my greatest weakness & fear was of the **big R – REJECTION.** Yep, you heard it right… as great, funny, cool and popular as I was and still am – my number one struggle was Rejection. I was scared people wouldn't like me, that I wasn't funny enough or even cool enough to be in the "popular in-crowd!" I guess the jokes were on me. This weakness and fear allowed me not to be as bold as I wanted to be in High School. Missed opportunities, missed and failed relationship/dating experiences, emptiness, and neglected jobs… all of these things happened because of my fear or weakness of Rejection. Thinking back on it now, I realized how great my impact and influence would have been if I wouldn't have been scared of what others would say.

At first I didn't think of it as a gift, and begged God to remove it. Three times I did that, and then he told me, My grace is enough; it's all you need. My strength comes into its own in your weakness. Once I heard that, I was glad to let it happen. I quit focusing on the handicap and began appreciating the gift. It was a case of Christ's strength moving in on my weakness. Now I take limitations in stride, and with good cheer, these limitations that cut me down to size—abuse, accidents, opposition, bad breaks. I just let Christ take over! And so the weaker I get, the stronger I become. [2 Corinthians 12:8-10]

I've learned something over the last few years that really has guided me when I feel rejection trying to creep up to the #1 spot — *'Even in my weakness, if I'm surrendered to Jesus, he still makes me Strong & when I'm in him, he never sees my weakness!'* What a thought… Are you telling me, I can struggle with my weakness, and Jesus still approves me? That's a ood question, and the answer is a great big **YES** // And He gives me strength in the midst of my weakness? **YES, and better yet, He will help you overcome this weakness!**

I have learned that in some areas I am weak. That in some situations, I am broken and frail. And guess what… I am okay with that. I know that Christ is my strength; therefore I can be weak. As a matter of fact, if I am in Christ, He **has** to be strong. Because my weakness would've killed me or depleted me to the point where I would have been taken out of the race.

Recently, I had a situation where I thought I was the "the one," but in actuality wasn't chosen. The very minute the news broke, the mindset [spirit] of rejection tried to set me back with what God was doing. Immediately, I found myself in intense prayer over the situation and taking my mind captive to the negative thoughts. Needless to say, I was actually okay with the decision and am content in it. Here, I took another rejection situation, but instead of allowing it to beat me for a few days – I focused on the positives and Jesus' strength in my life.

I've developed a joy in leaning on Jesus' strength, especially when it comes to ministry and preaching/teaching. When I started in full-time ministry, I used to be afraid of networking with other youth pastors I didn't know or preaching before large crowds. Now, that my joy in the strength of Jesus outweighs the frailty of my weakness… I like and enjoy networking with other pastors/leaders and speaking to the large crowds. It literally all boiled down to this – I would rather be rejected before man… then to be rejected by God.

Take a look at your life and see where you are weak! It's in your weakness, the Lord is trying to accomplish the greatest victory for your life. YOU ARE WEAK, but because HE IS STRONG… YOU STILL GET THE VICTORY! I love how *The Message* paraphrased version of the Bible puts the scripture above… ***My strength comes into its own in your weakness.*** This just means that His strength and power is made perfect when we are weak and rely on him alone. I'm weak… and that's okay cause my strength is not in me but in Christ!

The Pain that Change

Over the years of ministry and life, I have faced the dreaded pain that is a part of life. The Pain of death, failure, betrayal, loneliness, and lack. This pain cuts deep but was a part of the process, that God has me on. Pain is a part of leadership. It's also an unfortunate part of life. You and I will face pain at some point in our businesses, ministries, relationships, and daily lives. I am willing to bet that those who are reading this right now are going through some type of painful situation or circumstance. It's a reality that must work its course. If you are drawing breath right now, you will go through some kind of pain.

It's not easy to deal with, but it is needed for the journey God wants to take us on. It teaches us wisdom, resiliency, faith, hope, and to have tough skin. The necessity of pain is shaped by our experiences in life. Pain doesn't just show up for no reason; it's a sure sign that something needs to change. Pain comes in all different types of ways such as sickness (physical), depression (mental), abuse of any kind, death, loss of job/finances, relational struggles, etc.

We have all heard of the old sayings that "what doesn't kill us, only makes us stronger," and "pain is gain" — both are true and Biblical. A.W. Tozer says it this way about pain and trials of life:

"It is doubtful whether God can bless a man greatly until He has hurt him deeply."
- A.W. Tozer

If we try to run away from pain and don't surrender it to Jesus, we have robbed God from doing his job as a father and restorer. It is his pleasure to take all the hurt, pain, & brokenness and make it good, fruitful and beautiful. There was a man in the Bible who was all too familiar with pain, anguish, and the tears of life. This man found himself in a garden alone, after living a holy and blameless life, betrayed by a friend, pending denial of friendship and just tired. He spent that time in the garden crying and feeling the proverbial weight on his shoulders as he will soon carry the sins of mankind upon his back. Knowing fully well that his Father for a moment would turn his back on him and his impending death for a crime he did not commit was near. This man, of course, is Jesus and this reality surrounds his death by crucifixion. But it lends us first-hand experience into how to deal with pain.

Pain will either propel us to our destiny or cripple us in being stagnant… the choice in how we respond is solely ours. Jesus could have decided that he wasn't going to endure the cross (pain). He could have allowed his flesh and human nature to take over his deity. We know without any doubt, that if this decision were acted upon, Jesus would've never reached his full earthly potential and destiny. Earthly, in a sense to atone for sin as the perfect sacrifice, making us sons & daughters of God, the Father. The entire course of history would have changed at that moment, and with certainty, life as we know it would be different. Humanity would be guilty of all of our sins, without the blood-bought atonement of Jesus Christ. There would've been no propitiation of sin, no sacrifice, and no right-standing relationship with God. Your choice to "fight or flight" when it comes to pain will show your true colors and character. The entire course of history would have changed at that moment, and with certainty, life as we know it would be different. Your choice to "fight or flight" when it comes to pain will show your true colors and characters. Trust me, it's hard! But when we look that pain in the eye and face it head on — we enjoy walking with God to overcome it. I love how poetically 1 Peter 5:10 puts it in the *Amplified* translation of the Bible:

"After you have suffered for a little while, the God of all grace [who imparts His blessing and favor], who called you to His own eternal glory in Christ, will Himself complete, confirm, strengthen, and establish you [making you what you ought to be]."

Practical Ways to Deal with Pain

- **Identify** what or who caused the Pain — was it a boss, parent, friend, an ex, health issues, a death, an accident, yourself?
- **Seek to understand** how you can grow from the Pain — will I grow as a leader, employee, spouse, OR has this happened so that I can chase my dream or fulfill my purpose?
- **Honor the Pain** (probably the hardest part) — can you see the good in the Pain and/or even thank the person or thing that cause the pain? This is for you, and not the other person or situation.
- **MOVE FORWARD** — simply embrace the change and growth from the pain! Pray and rejoice in who God is shaping you to become.

2 Corinthians 4:16-18 | So we do not lose heart. Though our outer self is wasting away, our inner self is being renewed day by day. For this light momentary affliction is preparing for us an eternal weight of glory beyond all comparison, as we look not to the things that are seen but to the things that are unseen. For the things that are seen are transient, but the things that are unseen are eternal.

1 Peter 4:12-13 | Beloved, do not be surprised at the fiery trial when it comes upon you to test you, as though something strange were happening to you. But rejoice insofar as you share Christ's sufferings, that you may also rejoice and be glad when his glory is revealed.

2 Corinthians 7:8-11 | For even if I made you grieve with my letter, I do not regret it—though I did regret it, for I see that that letter grieved you, though only for a while. As it is, I rejoice, not because you were grieved, but because you were grieved into repenting. For you felt a godly grief so that you suffered no loss through us. For godly grief produces a repentance that leads to salvation without regret, whereas worldly grief produces death. For see what earnestness this godly grief has produced in you, but also what eagerness to clear yourselves, what indignation, what fear, what longing, what zeal, what punishment! At every point, you have proved yourselves innocent in the matter.

It's Worth It

Three hundred, that's 3-0-0 — 300 rejection emails. About five years ago, I wrote a blog and journal entry about Rejection being my biggest weakness or struggle and learning how to deal with it. Over these last five years, I had received 300+ emails (sitting in an email folder marked "I'm Weak, That's Okay") of rejection, with more than 50 coming since March 2016 when I resigned my pastoral position in Kalamazoo, MI. That is just emails and not including phone calls, unanswered or nonresponsive applications or snail mail. I think for me, what was hard to come to terms with is that while I know, "it's not personal, just business & ministry" — I still took it personally and felt the weight of it all. Moreover, while encouragement from friends and family was needed and useful, at times, it wasn't what I wanted at the moment. I was looking for someone to just respond beyond church rhetoric or Christianese and really see the hurt and struggle.

I would think to myself -- "If I hear another person say, 'well it wasn't meant to be, God has a better plan,' I'm literally going to go crazy. Duh! I am fully aware that God is in control AND I know what the Bible says. Why has the Church gone wrong with all this Christian 'pharisaical' babble? Whatever happened to weeping with those who mourn and laughing with those who laugh? Our job is to encourage, and not to say stupid things that really doesn't help people's situation. We cannot lose our compassion in an effort to hand out Bible verses. We have to be better listeners showing grace and love in how we respond. Without grace and love, these Bible verses are merely words on paper, filled with confused noise never reaching its full potential (1 Corinthians 13:1-2)."

I have come to grips that man's rejection only means that God has something bigger, better and beneficial for me! I have been in a season for a while where God has been teaching, renewing and redefining who He is as a Father and what true faith is.

Not this simple level of faith that we hear talked about but a deeper & stronger level of faith that is actually lived out.

I will remember March 2016 for the rest of my life. At the beginning of that month, I remember sitting at a conference table with 4 of my friends (some pastors and lead staff at a church in Michigan) letting them know of my resignation (due to things on their end) and feeling the sting, weight, and emptiness of leaving people I had grown to love. During those moments at the table, I was very emotional and had many questions, doubts about calling, loneliness, and uncertainty. These were people whom I had left my family and friends back in Atlanta, went broke to relocate, and became a part of their life. Their family and friends became mine, I engaged in their culture and trusted wholeheartedly. So, at that table, that day in March, all I could think about were these questions to God: "What was the purpose?", "Are we they yet?" and "What & where is the Good being worked out?"

That moment then has turned into this moment now as I flesh out this book in tears and retrospection! Same questions, same thoughts, and the same emotions. Through no fault of my own, I felt the full weight of rejection even though I wasn't rejected. It was an all too familiar pain that was genuinely crippling and now once again, I'm feeling the weight of it all and simply just tired. Rejection emails after another for ministry positions, I was well-qualified to do. Tired of the ups & downs, tired of the struggle, tired of the no's, tired of the pain… just tired!

This isn't a chapter in a book to get you and even myself into all the feels… just me expressing what's in my heart and getting it off of my chest so that we can overcome. In this, I feel like

Joseph. *A man who had a vision from the Lord but was rejected by his family and cast in a pit by his brothers.* He gets pulled out of the pit only to go into slavery and placed in short-lived prosperity as the head of the household of Potiphar, who's the captain of the guard in Pharoah's kingdom. The position is taken away from him through lies, and due to no fault of his own, he ends up in prison. In prison, after being initially rejected by a person he helped, he is remembered years later by him. Joseph interprets Pharoah's dream and finds favor with Pharoah. From there, he's faithfully propelled out of prison to the #2 person in charge of an entire kingdom and country who then saves the same family who rejected him as well as the whole country. The primary verse I got out of this reality of Joseph was this:

As for you, you meant evil against me, BUT GOD MEANT IT FOR GOOD, to bring it about that many people should be kept alive, as they are today. – Genesis 50:20

So, eagerly await God's promotion and trajectory into His glorious splendor he has for you. Until then, wait patiently with joyful courage, working on your character, learning life's lessons, continuing in love & grace speaking of Jesus. Psalm 105:19 says this, "Until the time came to fulfill his dreams, the LORD tested Joseph's character." Your character is what God is trying to test and grow. The call to more and elevation is found in the Night season! Endure the darkness in order to get to the Light. Joseph understood darkness... through the pit and the prison. Whatever you are going through trust that God is working out the details. If he promised it to you, know that his heart equals his hand. I can promise you this, that if Joseph's brother wouldn't have did what they did, Joseph's dream would have never came to pass. It is in the actions of his wicked brothers that cause an entire country to be saved including his brother. God will use all the pain and all the negative situation to bring about his fulfilled promise in your life.

So Joseph said to his brothers, "Come near to me, please." And they came near. And he said, "I am your brother, Joseph, whom you sold into Egypt... So it was not you who sent me here, but God. He has made me a father to Pharaoh, and lord of all his house and ruler over all the land of Egypt. – Genesis 45:4;8

And so, I said all this to say... I DON'T KNOW WHAT'S NEXT FOR YOU AND I. My trust is in that what & where ever the Lord leads, it will be **WORTH IT ALL**. Every pit, every prison experience, and every situation are worth it all in the grand scheme of things that the Lord has for us. *For he who promised is faithful!*

THE GREAT ARCHITECT

Unless the LORD builds the house, its builders labor in vain. Unless the LORD watches over the city, the watchmen stand guard in vain. In vain you rise early and stay up late, toiling for food to eat— for He grants sleep to those He loves. Psalm 127:1-2

For the past few months, I have been sensing the Lord stir something in the atmosphere. Back in 2011, I was speaking a few times on Psalms 127:1-2 and how God has an urgent need to build his Church. In August of that year, I had a dream about that same scripture (Psalm 127) that literally woke me up concerning what the Lord was doing. Without going into too many details about the dream, I was speaking at a really large youth/young adults conference for a dear friend of mine, with some other young prominent preachers and worship leaders. I vividly remember a complete shifting in the conference arena, as I stepped on stage after worship. After giving honor to the conference host (my friend) and having fun for a little while, I immediately stated that the Lord, sent me on "assignment" to bring an offense to the conference attenders, specifically the leaders who were there. That they had been vying for position and status in the eyes of the world and Christendom. That a lot of the people (leaders) were there to hear more from & "rub elbows" with the prominent leaders/singers, than from what God directly wanted to say to them. After saying this in my dream, I went into the context of my message which was on Psalms 127:1-2 and how we are building houses, God never required or asked us to build. Afterward, I gave a two-fold altar call and invitation; 1- for leaders to repent for vying for favorites and 2- for everyone else to surrender to the master builder!

Fast forward a few months later in November 2011 – I was sitting in a young adults' life group with some awesome people including my best friend who was in the dream, and I got this massive sense of heat all over me. We were discussing some changes in that ministry as well as where and what we see God doing next for us. My turn comes around, and I didn't say anything… as if I couldn't speak. Everyone else finished and as we were closing out for the night, I finally felt led to speak. I recall saying that the Lord is about to do some amazing things in our midst and that we as a ministry was about to a part of a revival in our city. I briefly shared with them on Habakkuk 3:2 and that the prayer of our hearts has to shift to seeing God revive things in our day now. That the past revivals, awakenings, and movements weren't good enough for now, we DESPERATELY NEEDED our own.

Now, this has brought me to a moment of realizing my feelings & sensing those same stirrings in the atmosphere years later. Stirrings of a season of intense prayer and seeking Jesus for the revival & movement that's about to take place in my life & ministry as well as in this generation, that only He can do. I find myself at the mercies of Psalms 127:1-2 once again, rendered over the fact that unless Jesus is the foundational architect of His house, we are wasting our time. A blunt but sincere and hopeful call to all believers from the Lord… *"Here's my rest; let me build."* More and more as I read, understand, and study my heart is overwhelmed and burden for the church to allow God to speak directly to us and stop "doing" church. We as leaders need to honestly carve out time in our day and week to wholeheartedly seek God for our families, friends, city, businesses, churches and nation/government. A time to honestly look forward to our encounters and experience with the Lord! In it, we fast and pray, worship, soak in God's presence speaking only when necessary. Us, being fully present for our time with God, is enough… so words aren't always required because God knows our heart but desires our time and attention. That doesn't mean he doesn't want to hear our voice. He delights in hearing our unique voice as his son or daughter. It just means, we are more focus on enjoying him and listening to his voice and heart.

The beauty of Psalm 127 is that the Lord, our God is the one building his house. He is the one watching over the city. As if to say, he is the perfect builder and watchmen. I genuinely believe that this scripture in context is talking not about brick and mortar buildings but the real you, as a person. We are the house (temple) of the Holy Spirit. We are that city on a hill. I find it interesting that Jesus' earthly occupation was that of a carpenter. I also find it interesting that one of Jesus' names in scripture is the Chief Cornerstone and so surprising that the builders rejected him (Psalm 118:22-23; Matthew 21:42-44). The Great Architect desires your nearness so that you can rest as he builds your life. No need to strive, toil, worry or fret. His master plan is perfect, and so is his timing. He never needs more time for the renovation. Believe it or not, you are his most beautiful masterpiece and award-winning design. When he looks at you and watches over you, you are the apple of his eye whom he finds lovely as you reflect his radiance. Over the years this has been a learning process for me as I "think" I know what is best for my life. I am learning that only in his time, will perfection be made in and through me. And that's my prayer for you. Rest and enjoy God as he does the work!

In their heart's humans plan their course, but the
LORD establishes their steps. -Proverbs 16:9

I felt the Lord speaking this to me as I was in intentional prayer and "daddy time" with my heavenly father:

Man is building his house in which he wants God to furnish
for man's sake. All the while God is desiring to build His
House and furnish it for man's sake. HIS (Jesus) work can
NEVER become OUR work until we surrender to Him &
wait at His feet. Then are we able to become co-laborers
with Christ… receiving the call as son or daughter.

Stay encouraged my friend and know that God is NOT done with you yet. The mere fact that you are reading this, and drawing breath are significant indicators that his plan for your life is more than you can think. Tenderly wait on him, with all the joy of heaven cheering for you!

DON'T DO IT ALONE

When we learn to live life-on-life with other people
and truly partner together, we are able to go further.
#DontDoItAlone #TeamWork @meCoreyG

Lately, I have been thinking a lot, more than I would like to admit about what's biblical relationship (friendship & community) and even evaluating some of my personal relationships. True friendship demands relationship. Trust is essential to true friendship for we all need someone with whom we can share our lives, thoughts, feelings, and frustrations. We need to be able to share our deepest secrets with someone, without worrying that those secrets & inner thoughts are blasted everywhere! Failing to be trustworthy with those intimate secrets can destroy a friendship, with the quickness. Faithfulness and loyalty are the keys to true friendship. Without them, we often feel betrayed, left out, and lonely. In true friendship, there is no backbiting, no negative thoughts, no turning away. True friendship pushes both parties to be and do greater. True friendship requires certain accountability & openness. This friendship encourages one another and forgives one another where there has been offense. Genuine friendship supports during times of struggle, failure, and success. They know how to weep when one is weeping and celebrate when one is celebrating.

One of the greatest biblical accounts of this true friendship is found in 1 Samuel 18, talking about the authentic relationship between David and Jonathan. These two men truly cared for each other and had great trust and confidence in one another. Listen to the language of 1 Samuel 18:1-5

"As soon as he had finished speaking to Saul, the soul of Jonathan was knitted to the soul of David, and Jonathan loved him as his own soul. And Saul took him that day and would not let him return to his father's house. Then Jonathan made a covenant with David, because he loved him as his own soul. And Jonathan stripped himself of the robe that was on him and gave it to David, and his armor, and even his sword and his bow and his belt. 5 And David went out and was successful wherever Saul sent him, so that Saul set him over the men of war. And this was good in the sight of all the people and also in the sight of Saul's servants."

This type of friendship was more in-depth than just buddies hanging out. Jonathan treated David as if he was his own brother, not only welcoming him into his home, but he also gave him gifts and clothes off of his own back (literally). Their friendship was tested when Saul, Jonathan's father wanted to kill David. Jonathan believed in the innocence of David and helped him escape the wrath of King Saul. Jonathan risked his own life for David, who was a fugitive to King Saul. Love compelled him to act, even at the chance of punishment and even death. Jonathan deserves a lot of credit in the narrative of King David. Their relationship was so connected that King

David honors his best friend Jonathan by sparing Jonathan's crippled son, Mephibosheth life. Not only does King David gives the entire inheritance of Saul (Mephibosheth's grandfather) to Mephibosheth but he also brings him (his family, and servants) into the palace to live out the rest of his years as a part of the royal family of King David, eating at the table of the King. (2 Samuel 9)

I've too noticed something reading this scripture. David, who would eventually become King David, would've never stepped into his divine purpose unless Jonathan was willing to call him into his own life. This gets me thinking about my own life and the "friends" I have developed in my life. I think about those who I could clearly identify as my Jonathan and those who I play Jonathan in their life. And if I am honest with myself, I can clearly identify about 3 authentic [ministry] relationships where this plays out and about 5 other relationships [outside of ministry]. Some may say that's not a lot, but I'm reminded of Jesus who only had 3 in his inner circle as close confidants. I've shared all this to get to the main point for you... Cultivate Authentic Relationships!

I believe the church (us individually and as a corporate body together) is at a crucial time where authentic relationship must be built & cultivated. Kingdom minded people coming together for Jesus' purpose. God is fostering relationships with people who will not just speak a good word but put it with actions. Jonathan told David that his love for him was great, but he proved it with his actions. Strategic relationships are being born so God's vision can go forth. One will carry the vision in thought and voice while one will run with it so it can be implemented/fulfilled (Habakkuk 2:2-3). In these last days will prove the ones who are willing to risk their own life (of desires, comfort, and resources) for the betterment and progress of the church body and its members. The time for fake and unintentional friendship is over. There is a cry from a hurting generation that is longing and looking for willing ones to befriend them and move forward in God's redemptive purpose. Build a solid friendship around you...

Tag Teaming the Dream

When my brother and I were younger *(and even somewhat now)*, we were avid Wrestling fans. We *(and our cousins too)* would imitate all the legends... I mean Sting, Ric Flair, Randy Savage *(RIP)*, Bret Hart, Hulk Hogan, Triple H, The Rock, and Stone Cold Steve Austin. We were totally obsessed. And if I can be brutally honest, it was through the grace of God and a praying mother that we are still alive from performing some of the dangerous moves we would see on tv or at live events in Atlanta.

> *Disclaimer: When the TV Screen says*
> *"DON'T TRY THIS AT HOME" ... it*
> *literally means that! Word to the wise!!!*

Some of our classic matches, the ones that were memorable and dear to us were when we would create or imitate a *stable* with our cousins and friends. Now a stable in wrestling terms means a team/group united in vision. My stable was called *D-Pac,* and my brother's was called *Threat. I know... silly but work with me.* My team was united in vision, that as their leader, I was going to become the World Heavyweight Champion and as a team, we were going to become the Tag Team Champions... *and YES, for those of you wondering – our team won.* Success! I knew that if I wanted to accomplish my goals and become the World Heavyweight Champion and Tag Champs, I was going to have to surround myself with some people, who understood the importance of allying and working together. Some of the most dominant, creative and talented wrestlers were a part of tag teams or stables. As a matter of fact, a majority of them improved and were better because of this "elite" group of men uniting for their championship goal.

This gets me thinking… *what if our ministries were like this?* Where we as the leader of the team [Pastor, Life Group Leader, Business Owner, coach, parent, etc.] would develop our teams appropriately to accomplish one goal… yet not our goal, but Jesus' goal? As a pastor, I began to think - *What if we fashion our ministries to work as a team and we really start tag teaming on Satan? What if our World Heavyweight Championship match was Preaching Jesus with authority and passion to this lost generation? And our Tag Team Championship match was teaming up with parents to nurture and disciple their children so that they could win in and at life.*

All wrestling aside… we are in an epic struggle were the familiar faces of our generation are fading away and lost. We need leaders in every sphere of influence, who will get out of the way, stop trying to do life alone and team up with other leaders and fight for these young people. Leaders willing to fight for their businesses, government agencies, school systems and the family unit. Leaders that will get before God and beg him to send them men & women who have His vision, His heart, and His grace so that His Church is built, His Kingdom expanded, Jesus' name glorified, and people set free to live abundantly. This applies to all context of leadership. If you are a leader in your business, at school or just in your home, be bold to develop a team of people who are passionate about Jesus, your success and the success of the content. DON'T DO IT ALONE!

Three simple things to remember... Pray for a Team, Build the Team, Invest in the Team.

Pray for a Team: Carve out time to wholeheartedly pray and seek God for the leaders who would be on your team. Begin searching for those who would add to the team, making it better. Look beyond the resume and skill set. Please make sure the chemistry, character traits and credibility are actively present in their life.

Build the Team: When God reveals the people for this team, begin to place them in the right area. Look for their gifts and talents. Ask them about their passions! Understand your needs and the needs of your people. You might have the right people for your team, but they're placed in the wrong position or role. Make the necessary changes that benefit them, the group and the organization.

Invest in the Team: Pour into them your time, resources, prayers, and energy... making sure they are well nourished. Investing in the team can take a lot of the leader, but it is often overlooked even when you have a high-capacity team. Don't micromanage them but definitely set expectations and evaluate progress. Allow the team to fail forward and grow as they work together.

Throughout the Bible, God has always used team ministry to further his Kingdom. Adam/Eve, Moses/Aaron, Joshua/Caleb, Elijah/Elisha/Jehu, Mary/Martha, Jesus & His Disciples (and even with the 12, Jesus still had an inner core team of 3 with Peter, James, & John), all the Apostles together and so on.

We were not called into ministry to act alone. We are not meant to be alone in life. I'm not talking about so-called "friends" we only see when the latest "Big" conference is in town or our online social media... but the authentic relationships with people in **our** context and city that are willing to sacrifice and dig the trenches with us for our community.

Look at what Solomon had to say about being alone in ministry & life:

---

7 I turned my head and saw yet another wisp of smoke on its way to nothingness: 8 a solitary person, completely alone-no children, no family, no friends-yet working obsessively late into the night, compulsively greedy for more and more, never bothering to ask, "Why am I working like a dog, never having any fun? And who cares?" More smoke. A bad business. 9 It's better to have a partner than go it alone. Share the work, share the wealth. 10 And if one falls down, the other helps, but if there's no one to help, tough! 11 Two in a bed warm each other. Alone, you shiver all night. 12 By yourself you're unprotected. With a friend you can face the worst. Can you round up a third? A three-stranded rope isn't easily snapped. Ecclesiastes 4:7-12 MSG

Invest. Invest. Invest

You have a group of people who have the same heart as you do for business or ministry. They all have great personalities and characteristics. Some are artistic/creative while others are thinkers. Some are funny, and some are serious. They're willing, motivated and eager for the challenge ahead…. Now, what? **INVEST** in them! If you can see yourself doing life with them, **invest** in them. If you see yourself working with them for the next 5-10 years, **invest** in them and their families.

This to me is definitely on my top leadership philosophy. Too often young leaders try to do it all by themselves and are the lone ranger… which is very dangerous especially in ministry & business! A great leader is only as great as the team of people around them. I wholeheartedly believe in a team approach in business and ministry. I am willing to invest in the men and women around me to effectively leverage the individual gifts God has given them to expand God's Kingdom. When I as the leader am willing to invest in their success, we both win. This is called synergy. When I want to cultivate my team, I am willing to go out of my way to nourish them.

This is 100% modeled by Jesus with his disciples, especially Peter, James, and John….

How many times did Jesus use simple parables to show them the Kingdom of Heaven? Or how about how many times did Jesus invite Peter & the Sons of Thunder (James & John) to intimate fellowships/journeys with him? These weren't just times of play and innocent chatter, it was the very moments that shaped these men lives after Jesus' ascension into heaven. Jesus used everyday moments to teach and invest in His follower's life. If you want your teams to be successful even to the point to where you are not there… invest in them. Invest your time, energy, money, resource, wisdom and knowledge. Often times you will never know the effectiveness of your investment on them until you aren't there, and they must step up to the plate.

THE REMEMBERING GOD

"And God remembered _____! #YouAreTheBlank #JesusFocusedLife" - @meCoreyG

Crazy to think that the God who created the entire universe merely with just his voice and the one who shaped humankind with his hands then gently kneeing to bless and release life with his breath, wants or needs to remember. If you're like me, you will find this amusing at the bare least yet this phrase **"And God remembered..."** is found at least six times throughout scripture. That's six times the Abba God remembered what he said or promised. All were concerning his people (the faithful believers) who were downcast in spirit, in trouble and needing a righteous savior or needing mercy extended to them. I wonder if the reason God remembers is simply the fact that God wants to remind us also. Remind us that we are not forgotten, left alone, abandoned or without mercy and grace. Maybe his remembering is a sign that he actually cares for our soul and yearns to bless us. As a natural father hopefully remembers his children, how much greater and more significant is the Heavenly Father to remember us. This happened to me personally in August of 2017. I was in a very dry season in ministry and life. I felt like I was done with ministry altogether and literally screamed at God. I was tired and done. The proverbial saying of "stick a fork in him, he's done" would have been appropriate for my heart and mind. Vividly I remember on the morning of August 22, 2017, waking up physically tired from lack of sleep the night before. I went through my normal day and at 6:01 pm, I received this text from one of my best friends, Pastor Johnathan Key:

Also!! I received a word for you early this morning and forgot to tell you… it was a reminder that God's heart for you hasn't changed."

That was spot on and totally what I needed to hear. That through all my lack, "feeling" like a failure, "feeling" abandoned by God… The uncreated God looks down on me, hears my prayers and speaks tenderly to me through my friend, just to remind me that **HIS HEART** hasn't changed for me. Even as I am writing these chapters months later, I am fighting back emotions in a coffee shop. 7+ billion people on earth, and just for that one moment in time it felt like I was the only one God was thinking of specifically… by name.

Could it be that you are reading this right now because the Lord has perfectly set up this Kairos moment so that he could remind you that he is fighting for you? This one chapter could be a reminder to you that God sees you, hears you and is answering your heart's desire. That just like me, his heart hasn't changed for you. Let me prophetically speak to your heart and mind: **GOD IS THE REMEMBERING GOD**

- Are you feeling hopeless and confined? - **God remembered Noah and all the animals**. Genesis 8:1 ~ *"But God remembered Noah and all the beasts and all the livestock that were with him in the ark. And*

God made a wind blow over the earth, and the waters subsided.

- Married couples, are you wanting a child? - **God Remembered Rachel AND Hannah**. Genesis 30:22-23 - *"Then God remembered Rachel, and God listened to her and opened her womb. She conceived...*

  1 Samuel 1:19-20 - *They rose early in the morning and worshiped before the LORD then they went back to their house at Ramah. And Elkanah knew Hannah his wife, and the LORD remembered her. And in due time Hannah conceived...*

- Are you walking in obedience and fleeing that which God told you to leave? - **God Remembered Abraham and Lot.** Genesis 19:22 - So *it was that, when God destroyed the cities of the valley, God remembered Abraham and sent Lot out of the midst of the overthrow when he overthrew the cities in which Lot had lived.*

- Are you desperately in need of mercy? - **God remembered Ephraim.** Jeremiah 31:20 -

  Is Ephraim my dear son? Is he my darling child? For as often as I speak against him, I do remember him still. Therefore my heart yearns for him; I will surely have mercy on him, declares the LORD.

- Do you have God's promises over/for your life that has not been answered yet? - **God remembered his promise and covenant with Abraham.** Psalm 105:42 - For *he remembered his holy promise, and Abraham,* *his servant. More verses* - Psalm 106::45 | Psalm 111:5 | Luke 1:72-79

There is more than what you can see. God has already gone before you and is reminding you to stay faithful and trust in him. God is leading you somewhere. Though the process might be long and tiring, it is for your benefit and blessing. Remember the people of Egypt and God leading them out of bondage.

When Pharaoh finally let the people go, God DID NOT LEAD them along the main road that runs through Philistine territory, even though that was the SHORTEST route to the Promised Land. God said, "If the people are faced with a battle, they might change their minds and return to Egypt." — Exodus 13:17 New Living Translation

---

Sometimes the shortest distance and timeframe is not the best. A wise person once said, *"if it's easy to obtain, it's easy to lose."* If the people would have gone on the main road (shortest distance) towards the promised land, they would have been easier to spot from Pharaoh… hence face opposition and return to slavery. Often times, the waiting process or journey proves the character and integrity not just of the person, but of the calling.

Our calling is worth the extra mile… worth not shortcutting or cheating our way, worth the necessary process, and worth the learning experiences. We have a God who will lead us and direct our path. Trust the narrow road he has us on. For you and me, Psalm 16:11 & Psalm 37:4-5 proves so true, in times of doubt, struggle and taking the "main road" of life.

This reminds me of my favorite poem by Robert Frost entitled *The Road Not Taken*. I love how even in Robert's poem at the end he says, *"Two roads diverged in a wood, and I— I took the one less traveled by, and that has made all the difference."* This man is faced with a decision to either go where few have been or trot down the beaten path. His decision was to choose the road that only a few have gone, and for him, that made all the difference.

Whatever journey in life you are on… know that God is with you and he has you on the best path for your benefit and for his glory. He remembers his plans over your life. He knows your value and knows your worth. You are not forgotten for God remembers you.

FAITH THAT SPEAKS

Some miracles will only happen when you step out in faith and trust the God of Miracles! - @meCoreyG

Not going to lie… the F-word, faith has always scared me and often makes me wonder about the mysteries of God. This word FAITH is a word that often gets shouted and preached from the platform, quoted (through Scriptures) and handed out like candy when things go wrong. Lastly, without delay it seems to be lacking in the actual time of need for it. Most people walking earth really don't know what faith is all about. We settled for the surface level of the meaning without a deep understanding of how to apply it to our lives and only live in it daily. By no means do I claim to understand it fully but through the grace of God and the journey the Lord has had me in the last 14 years of my life… I can say I have a pretty thorough knowledge of it. And if we are not careful, we will think faith is merely about us and not about God and his will.

Let's start with some basics of the idea and doctrine called Faith

Faith is not a magical wish, spell or thought

Faith is not a promise that you will always get what you have faith in or for

Faith is not a quick fix

Faith is the pleasure of God, specifically Abba, Father. (Hebrews 11:6)

Faith is hope beyond what normal eyes see, and minds believe (Hebrews 11:1)

Faith is trusting God no matter the circumstances or season of life (Proverbs 3:5-6)

Faith is a bestowed gift from God (Ephesians 2:8-9)

Faith takes work and is work (James 2:14-26)

Faith is a lifestyle (2 Corinthians 5:7, 2 Thessalonians 1:3)

Faith is a Fruit of the Spirit (Galatians 5:22)

Faith is a Spiritual Gift given by God to some

Faith is a Spiritual Gift given by God to some Christians for the common good (1 Corinthians 12:7-9)

Often times, if we are honest with ourselves and God, we view faith as this magical "genie-in-the-bottle" moment where we ask God for anything, and he has to give it to us. We hold so tightly the very thing we want and then when it doesn't come, we are upset and withdrawn. This is a very poor, inaccurate and even unbiblical view on faith. Faith was never meant to be a quick fix. Faith was never intended to be wishy-washy hope.

I wish I had the time to tell you everything in the last fourteen years of my life and ministry. If I did, I would have a bare minimum of three full-length books. I'll spare you the details and focus on the last three years. In my 32 years of life, I have never had to battle and struggle with faith like I had to in the previous three years. Where it seemed like it is taking forever to get to the promised land and destination that I know God has for me. The very place faith was calling me towards and place of expectation. I briefly shared this in the previous chapter on pain, if there were ever a story in the Bible that my life resembles the most it would be life and journey of Joseph. Seasons of asking God, "Are we there, yet?" Waiting in the meantime of life and seemingly going the longest distance to get to where I wanted to be. Moment of betrayal, being lied to and about and sabotaged. All that would make for an excellent movie. As I find myself in the throes of the struggle, I am often reminded of Psalm 105:19 *"Until the time came to fulfill his dreams, the Lord tested Joseph's character."* Could it be that in our waiting... the Lord is testing our character, testing our endurance and testing our faith. Maybe instead of Joseph's name, it's your name... you are the blank.

Until the time came to fulfill their dreams, the Lord tested _____'s character.

About a year ago, I was doing some personal study and a verse in the Bible jumped out at me. It literally felt like the Lord opened my eyes to the scripture. A familiar story about Pharaoh & the people of God (Exodus 13:17) but a verse I never really paid attention to until that day. Here's what the shocking verse says:

*When Pharaoh finally let the people go, God **did not lead** them along the main road that runs through Philistine territory, even though that was the **shortest** route to the Promised Land. God said, "If the people are faced with a battle, they might change their minds and return to Egypt."* – Exodus 13:17, New Living Translation

Notice that it was God's intention and doing to have them go a different direction. This wasn't because of sin or a mistake on their maps. The Lord sent them this long direction to cause their faith in him to increase. Gods concern was not the distance or timeframe in which they got to the promised land but their hearts condition when they got there. His main concern was them.

I wonder how easy it would have been for the people of Israel to take the main road. How much time would it have saved them? I often think about how easy it is for us today to go the simple and easy route in life. Life usually presents us with two choices – the choice of ease and less resistance or the choice of risk and pressure. Faith requires risk — the risk of failure, embarrassment, difficulty, and loneliness.

All through scripture (Psalms 16:11; Psalm 37:4; Proverbs 3:5-6, Matthew 6:25-34) God is calling his people to trust him and have faith that he will take good care of them as a good father does. Trust God and have faith even in the unknown and uncertainty of life. RISK IT ALL IN FAITH

While I was studying and reading this portion of scripture, I felt the Holy Spirit speak clearly to me – "Often times, the waiting process or journey proves the character and integrity not just of the person, but of the calling."

How true of this, in the season of life I am in… that God would use this little verse to speak in huge volumes to me that my faith, calling and purpose is worth the wait? If you and I were to get real, we give up way too quickly. Our faith in the very things God has promised us is lacking. We lose trust in God, ultimately not pleasing him. We quit knocking on the door of Heaven, quit being persistent, and quit going before the throne room of God. We need to remember that the faith that God has so beautiful bestowed upon us as a gift is the very thing that moves his heart towards action. Can we be found like the widow who sought for justice persistently from the hard judge (Luke 18:1-6) ... will faith be found not just on earth when the Son of Man (Jesus) returns but also in our own heart and mind? May we never waver in our faith. May we never stop going after the things of God. May our faith increase day by day.

One of my favorite Bible verses in all of Scripture is found in Hebrews 11:4, surrounding the life of Abel. The reflected story alone will get you in the feels, but the language the writer of Hebrews uses is so profound that it gets me thinking. Just ponder on the words:

---

*By faith Abel offered to God a more acceptable sacrifice than Cain, through which he was commended as righteous, God commending him by accepting his gifts. **And through his faith, though he died, he still speaks**. (HCSB)*

I have been marinating on that last part of the scripture lately – "And through his faith, though he died, he still speaks." Could this be said of me? Could I have a faith so strong, withstanding and battle-tested that years after I am dead and gone, still speaking to those who are alive? Abel was killed in Genesis 4, gets an honorable mention in both Hebrews 11 (v. 4) and Hebrews 12 (v. 24) and now today in this book. We are still speaking of the faith that he had. Abel never utters one word in the Bible. The exact knowledge of the faith he had in which we can pinpoint to is somewhat unknown. Abel is speaking to us today... can you hear him? His blood is crying out to a generation that says "your faith is worth it, live in it!" Beloved, you and I are bestowed one of the most important gifts we could ever give back to God – the gift of faith. Abel understood this and as such was the first person in the history of the world to be blessed and accredited for this gift of faith. Through all of history and what is to come, the faith of Abel will never be taken from him and always be made known. No matter who or what the Cain (haters, evil-doers, problems) in your life try to do - your faith in God must stand firm.

In all we do… if we truly want to live a Jesus focused life, we must learn to live, love and lead in faith. Faith breaks the chains of fear, unlocks to doors of complacency, and thrusts us forward into our future as we live on purpose for God.

I wonder what or who awaits you on the other side of your faith. May we never graduate from the University of Faith that teaches us to grow closer to God and closer to our own promised land.

ACKNOWLEDGMENTS

To my family – Eugene (dad) and Mary (mom), thank you for your constant support and encouragement. Thanks for raising Aaron and me in the ways of the Lord and instilling in us a strong foundation. I am the man and leader today because of the way you raised me. Thanks for the prayers and ministry conversations. Thanks for always supporting and believing in me. To my brother Aaron "Show," though you are no longer here, your faith and encouragement still speak (Hebrews 11:4) … thanks for believing in me. I am honored to carry the legacy of our family. To all my aunts and uncles as well as cousins and grandmothers – thank you for your love, support, and encouragement.

The Davis' boys - Jason (Desola), Philip and Brandon (Katie) - Thank you all for always having my back and supporting me through a lot of difficult and joyful seasons of life. Thanks for encouraging me to continue to pursue God and the many devotions we had when we were younger. Shout out to your dad - Adrian, and mom – Donna Pettigrew. Thanks for the always needed word of wisdom and encouragement.

To my Best Friends - Jordan Sharrett (Nikki) and Johnathan Key (Andrea) - Thank You! Thank you for supporting me in many seasons of life. Eternally grateful for all that you have done in public and behind the scenes privately. Heaven only knows the full impact that each of you has on my life and ministry. You are my brothers and sisters. Thank you for the Jonathan/David relationship I have with you all. *Jordan & Nikki*, thank you for standing with me when no one else did besides family. Thanks for believing in me and giving me hope when I was all out. I still have the tear-stained letter you wrote Nikki when I moved away in 2013, as a simple reminder as my sister. I cannot express with dry eyes what you guys have meant to me over the last nine years. *Johnathan & Andrea*, thank you for the laughs, tough but honest conversations (even at 2 am sitting in your driveway) and opening your home to me. So glad to be blunce to my nephew, Israel. Words could not express what you two have meant to me the last five years. #SaltNPepper

The Owen Family - Jason, John-Anthony (Caris), Julian (Keshia), Joel, Thank you for taking a risk on me 14 years ago when I was very "green" in ministry. We have done life together for over 18 years, and it is a blessing to know this family. I am honored to have been a part of a lot of the good moments in life as well as the most challenging ones. Posthumously thanks to Janine A. Owen - thank you for being a supportive spiritual mother to me. Though you are no longer here on earth, your faith still speaks from Heaven to me (Hebrew 11:4). Thanks for running your race and now cheering your boys (including me) on in our race.

SPECIAL THANKS

A special thanks to some pastors and leaders who have invested in me over the years from afar. Chad Veach, Christine Caine, Francis Chan, Jentezen Franklin, Judah Smith, Priscilla Shirer, and Robert Madu; Thank you for speaking volumes into my ministry via social media, leadership resources and messages.

John & Catherine Throneberry, Tyler & Julia Eads, Alliyah Harden, Ezra & Kate Cataldo, and Matthew & Hannah Overman – Thanks for being friends who are supportive, encouraging and faithful. Each of you believes in me and the ministry that comes through me. Forever grateful for our friendship and being family.

Gateway Church (Suwanee, GA) - Thank you all for being my home church. I came to you in a season of brokenness and uncertainty, and you welcomed me with opened arms allowing me to be a part of the family. Thanks for loving me, sending me out and blessing me every time I come home. Glad to be a part of this amazing church family and to be a part of the entire Sharrett's family lives. I am the leader today because I came under your ministry and leadership. Forever grateful, forever blessed, forever family.

Gateway Church (Shelbyville, TN) - So many amazing and wonderful friends who support and believe in me. People I can call family. Thank you, Pastor Jason & Sylvia Daughdrill, for taking a chance on me and giving me hope again to live my dream. *"Nothing will be wasted!"* While I can't name every fantastic family, I do want to mention five: Corey Voss, Dan & Jen Bucker, Chuck & Amanda Bynum, Donavan & Hosanna Haughton, Tammy Quick. Each of you has made a significant impact on my life and treated me like family. Lots of laughs, games, deep conversations and food. Thank you for believing in me and pushing me to my dreams.

Victory World Church (Norcross, GA) - My foundation, spiritual growth, and knowledge came from this church and the ministry of my former Youth Pastor Billy and Maribeth Humphrey. Victory was the place I fell back in love with Jesus and received salvation, water baptism, and baptism of the Holy Spirit. The church where I first became a leader/servant and the first church I preached in (as a youth). Thank you, Senior Pastors Dennis and Colleen Rouse. Forever grateful for the ministry of this church and your willingness to end the divide of racism in the church and community of Atlanta.

BOOK PASTOR COREY

Thank you for your inquiry into Pastor Corey's availability to speak at your event or service. It's a tremendous honor that you want to invite Corey to come to speak. If you would like to have Corey come and speak at your church service or event, leadership event, school campus, or other types of setting, don't hesitate to contact us. For more information, please email booking@coreygibson.org or visit www.coreygibson.org

COACHING: LEAD
WELL NETWORK

One of my passions is to pour into the next generation of leaders so that they can lead the charge. Being in ministry now 14 years as a pastor, speaker/evangelist, and creative I have learned a lot. I've learned a lot about leadership, growth, branding, and ministry life as a whole. I want to take everything I have learned all these years and invest them into other young leaders. As a part of this mentorship/coaching network, I will spend time coaching, counseling, consulting and encouraging leaders to remain fruitful and faithful.

As a part of this, you as a leader will get:

- One-on-One mentorship session (in-person, phone/text or FaceTime/Skype)
- Leadership sessions for the whole team (in-person or FaceTime/Skype)

- Monthly leadership emails and blogs
- Access to leadership resources (documents and procedures)

Leadership sessions and resources will cover:

- Ministry life & personal/family life
- How to communicate, preach & teach
- Creative branding/rebranding (social media, apps, and website)
- Building sustainable ministries
- Building strategic partners
- Recruiting, training and leading volunteers
- BIG picture and Vision Casting
- plus much more.

SOCIAL MEDIA & WEBSITES

Instagram, Facebook, Twitter - @mecoreyg

www.coreygibson.org (non-profit) | www.mecoreyg.com (personal & journals site)

Printed in the United States
By Bookmasters